PARK TREASURE

"Himma Finds Her Favorite Tree."

HIMMA LYNN ESTESS

To order additional copies of this book, contact:
Xlibris
1-888-795-4274
www.Xlibris.com
Orders@Xlibris.com

PARK TREASURE

"Himma Finds Her Favorite Tree."

HIMMA LYNN ESTESS

For
Felipa

Over
the Mud

Past
the Playground

Past
the Seats

Behind
the Baseball field

Around
More mud

There
You are

At
The Place.

Himma Lynn Estess

Age 7

Dunlavy Park

Around the corner from her home at

1512 Bonnie Brae St.

Printed in the United States
By Bookmasters